DOVER
THEN & NOW
IN COLOUR

PAUL WELLS & JEFF HOWE

The
History
Press

First published in 2012

The History Press
The Mill, Brimscombe Port
Stroud, Gloucestershire, GL5 2QG
www.thehistorypress.co.uk

ISBN 978 0 7524 8104 3

Typesetting and origination by The History Press
Printed in India.

CONTENTS

ACKNOWLEDGEMENTS

The opportunity to offer a Then & Now narrative to Dover's story was too compelling for us both to pass up. It's been a couple of years since *Dover Past & Present* and this has given us time to reflect on how we put that bumper collection of old pictures together. We hope that you will enjoy reading this second collection, which has given us as much pleasure compiling as the first did.

We were helped along the way by Bob and Kathleen Hollingsbee, the staff of Dover Museum and Dover Library, and they have our thanks. B. Pilgrim assisted us with the Promenade Pier and Pavilion Company, and we couldn't have done without the unswerving support of Sue and Jo. We are here because they are here.

ABOUT THE AUTHORS

Paul Wells is a local historian who leads history-based guided walks for the White Cliffs Countryside Project and English Heritage. He is also a committee member of the Western Heights Preservation Society.

As well as writing history articles for the local newpaper, Paul manages a number of websites including 'Great Mongeham Then and Now', 'Dover Then and Now' and 'Western Heights Today'. He lives in Deal, Kent.

Jeff Howe first started researching Dover's Western Heights Defences in 1991 and since then has gone on to give guided walks around the fortifications for the local authority and for English Heritage. A founding member of the Western Heights Preservation Society, formed in May 2000, Jeff is also a part-time history tutor for Kent County Council Adult Education, and is himself currently studying as a full-time history undergraduate.

INTRODUCTION

Dover was a busy, thriving place before the Second World War. Although there are few with first-hand experience of that conflict, it has been well documented. Books such as *Dover Past and Present*, published back in 2009, describe Dover's fascinating history during this era.

Many exciting changes to Dover have recently taken place or are under discussion. They include ferries at the Prince of Wales Pier, and cruise liners moored at the Admiralty Pier; a bright-red cable car sweeping down to the Wellington Dock shopping outlet and back up to the Western Heights; an elevator up the outside of the cliffs next to the restored Moats Bulwark; a national war memorial at the former Grand Shaft Barracks, along with a hotel and conference centre, accessible by a glass elevator that takes visitors up the centre of the Grand Shaft's staircase at walking pace whilst projections of Napoleonic troops walk up and down the three staircases carrying their backpacks and muskets.

If one ventures up the hill by foot, a Dover Discovery Ticket might soon allow you to explore the new heritage centre in the Drop Redoubt and weave your way through the moats and tunnels of the whole hillside, built to protect the town from attack. A three-day ticket will allow you access to all of the tourist attractions in Dover – including the Roman Experience, where you can see the painted bathhouse and Roman harbour, all under one magnificent glass roof.

Dover's 1970s tower block, Burlington House, is also due to be demolished, and a shopping mall built in its place. A new skywalk is also rumoured over the old dual carriageway. Terminal 2 will open, allowing traffic through only at night. A park-and-ride should further reduce traffic.

As you have probably gathered, this introduction does not describe the Dover of today. But if all current plans come to fruition, Dover could become a very different town. Never before has the town seen so many proposed regeneration projects, which could see Dover return to its former glory and become a World Heritage Site. There is nowhere as worthy of restoration as Dover. From Iron Age hillfort to cable cars on the Heights, Dover could soon be the town of the twenty-first century.

NO. 51 BIGGIN STREET

HERE WE HAVE a picture of not one but two of Dover's businesses: downstairs is Britcher's Bon Marché, the ladies' outfitters, and above is the Commercial Hotel. We're at 51 Biggin Street, and the Commercial Hotel was also next door at No. 50. Britcher's was there at least as early as 1928, but by about 1934 it had moved to No. 16 Cannon Street. No sign of it can be found by 1950. Bon Marché is French for 'good market' or 'good deal'. (There is no connection with the modern store of the same name.)

Before Britcher took the shop in Biggin Street it was the Singer Sewing Machine Co. The Central Temperance Hotel was at this site from 1912 to about 1921, though it was known as the Central Hotel between 1925 and 1969. The proprietor in the late 1920s was a Mr C. Watts.

CLAIRE'S ACCESSORIES HAS sprung up in nearly every major town and city in Britain. Its parent company was started in 1961 in Florida, USA and its headquarters are still there today. I wonder if the entrance mosaic is still there today under Claire's floor!

CENTRAL COMMERCIAL HOTEL.

LADIES OUTFITTERS

ARCHCLIFFE FORT

SET AGAINST THE sheer cliffs below the castle, Archcliffe Fort looks rather lost in the countryside, away from the hustle and bustle of the town. But opposite, just out of sight on this early photograph, is a military establishment which included a prison, an RASC (Royal Army Service Corps – today the Logistics Corps) yard and a set of married quarters. These were all permanent brick buildings.

In the centre of this picture is the north-east bastion of the fort, which was built in the later half of the seventeenth century. This is quite a rare piece of military architecture in Kent, as other forms of permanent fortifications were developed in the ensuing centuries. There were originally four bastions which jutted out from the fort, these designed to a plan known as the Angular Bastioned Trace: guns mounted on each bastion could provide cross-fire for each adjacent bastion.

MOST OF THE buildings opposite Archcliffe Fort were demolished in the 1960s to make way for industrial units. It was hoped that these would help to regenerate Dover and to create jobs. All but two of the military buildings were knocked down. One of these was a humble stable block which was used as a factory in the early 1960s by the newly arrived Metal Industries Ltd, the forerunner of the current Megger factory. The new factory, i.e. the building which we can see today, was built in 1965 and was officially opened by Earl Mountbatten in 1966.

The fort has changed much over the years. During the 1920s the seaward side was demolished to make way for an ever-expanding railway network. Despite the fact that the fort became a Scheduled Ancient Monument in 1979, the 'couvre port' or Barbican was demolished in 1991 to make way for the new A20 trunk road.

ATHOL TERRACE

IN THIS OLD photograph you're probably looking at Mr and Mrs Henry Albert Taylor and family. According to the 1901 census record, Henry and Emma lived here with their three sons and a daughter, along with a boarder, a Mr Leonard. Could this be he next to the couple standing in the doorway? It looks like the children are in the upstairs window – with maybe granny or the governess. Henry was a carpenter/joiner, and Mr Leonard may have had some connection to a golf club. The Taylors lived there until the late 1920s. Athol Terrace was built in the mid-nineteenth century and is Grade II listed.

THE TAYLORS COULD have walked but a few steps to the beach – which would have looked much like Shakespeare Beach does today. The building of the Eastern Arm Pier had begun a couple of years before. Today, we all suspect, there is probably little peace in this area.

The house is now derelict, although work has been started on it a couple of times. Maybe sometime in the near future those pretty bow windows might be replaced.

BIGGIN STREET

COULD IT BE that this photograph of T.R. Knighton's pork butcher's was taken for posterity due to the building's imminent demolition? This row of shops, next to the alley which was to become Priory Street, included Bowman's hairdresser's, Leigh's, who were engravers and cutlers, and Hadlow the plumber. These businesses were all there between at least 1905 and 1912. As you will notice, Bowman's hairdresser's is empty and the shop window is pasted up.

The row was in fact demolished to make way for a new post office building, which appeared in 1914. This, as you may recall, was itself demolished in 1998 to make way for a new Woolworths store.

WHO REMEMBERS WHEN Woolworths' premises were on the opposite side of Priory Street? You used to be able to enter the shop from the corner of Biggin Street and leave through doors in Worthington Street. When Woolworths left Dover, WHSmith took over that premises.

Woolworths came back to Dover in 1998 in a brand-new store, built on the footprint of the old post office. Unfortunately that famous brand, which dated back to Frank Woolworth's first store in Pennsylvania in 1879, came to an end in 2009, when severe financial difficulties struck. The site was quickly taken over by Peacocks, the value clothing retailer – which unfortunately has itself since gone into administration for the same reasons as Woolworths stores, although it has been rescued, for now, by another national chain.

13

MORE BIGGIN STREET

HERE'S A STREET scene just a little way up from the Metropole Hotel. Hatton was a draper and milliner trading from Nos 45-47 Biggin Street. His shop opened in 1896, and this date can be seen if you stop in the street and look up. Next door, at No. 48, the Maypole Dairy and the Welham Parker Teeth Manufacturer traded together, side by side. I suppose milk and teeth do go together! The gap in the buildings as we go up Biggin Street was filled in October 1911 by the King's Hall Cinema.

GEORGE HATTON'S SHOP finally closed for business in 1973. Nos 45-47 later became Dover Market Hall, then Lovell's, then John Menzies the stationer.

The BBC reported in May 1998: 'Margaret Beckett, the President of the Board of Trade, gave her blessing to the £68m takeover of John Menzies by WHSmith. The Minister made her decision after the Director General of the Office of Fair Trading advised her that the deal did not present any competition concerns.'

The shop that Thomson the travel agents now occupy was also part of the Hatton business. However, the premises is not part of the 1896 building, so perhaps Hatton had to expand as his business grew.

CANNON STREET

HERE WE SEE McDonald's, another manufacturer of teeth, Timothy White's Company Cash Chemists, and the Metropole Grocery and Provisions Stores. Alston the tailor was here too.

It is always an interesting exercise to walk down the oldest streets of Dover and look up. Some fantastic sights can be seen. The Metropole Hotel was as impressive a century ago as the Metropole Apartments are today. The original hotel dates to 1896 but it has seen many changes since those days. The Dover Motor Co. was here in 1915 and the Metropole Flats in 1939.

TODAY'S VIEW IS not that dissimilar, really. As we walk down Cannon Street we probably notice the Eight Bells public house, Subway café and the mobile-phone accessory shop – which still displays the 'Alston's' sign. You can see where the once-grand entrance to the hotel used to be, and it's a real shame that the shop where Timothy White's used to be is now empty. The Eight Bells was opened in 1997 and the old Metropole converted into flats or apartments in 2006. It had been empty and slowly decaying for fifteen years before being converted, and now contains a total of twenty-eight dwellings. The conversion was part of Kent County Council's 2005 'no use empty' campaign to bring disused properties back to life.

BROADLEES BOTTOM

THIS STRIKING VIEW of Dover Castle shows some areas with which we are all probably quite familiar: the keep, inner and outer curtain walls and the Norfolk towers to the right. Photographs of the castle taken from the east are also quite rare, come to think of it. The large mound to the left of the picture is Horseshoe Bastion, now totally obscured by trees. This was one of the bastions built in the 1790s during the Napoleonic Wars.

But what's more interesting are the huts in the foreground. These were built around 1920 and were probably officers' quarters. Interestingly they were each named after major battles of the First World War. They were, from furthest away, Messines, Ypres, Aisne, Marne and Mons.

TODAY THE TREES have taken over and not much of the original view is visible. Of the five huts that were originally built, only three remain. The one nearest us, Mons, was gone by 1960. The current hut or bungalow that occupies the space where Ypres stood (second furthest away) is a modern building. Unfortunately Ypres was a victim of shelling during the Second World War. In September 1944, during Dover's last shelling, Royal Artillery Sergeant T.E. Cook of the 216 Battery, 82nd Regiment, Light Anti-Aircraft Regiment was killed, along with several other townspeople – an attack which presumably also resulted in a direct hit on Ypres. Sergeant Cook is buried in Beckenham Crematorium and Cemetery.

THE FISHING FLEET

THIS PICTURE OF fishing vessels shows a scene probably long forgotten in Dover. None of the boats have registration markings, so dating this view is difficult. The Ordnance Quay and HM Gunwharf, home of the Army Pay Office, are on the right of this picture and show on a plan as 'Army

Ordnance Depot & Chief Paymaster's Offices'. This area is now a car park for Dover Harbour Board.

THIS PICTURE WAS taken in the autumn of 2011 when there were – conveniently – no boats in the dock. The basin had been allowed to go tidal, that is emptied of water, in order that the lock gates at the Wellington Bridge might be repaired. This is good news for us as it affords a good view of its layout.

The nearest building along the quayside was previously Dover Yacht Co. and is now Cullins Yard restaurant, and most recently the only microbrewery in the area was established in an adjacent former workshop.

CAMBRIDGE TERRACE

DOCTOR BEST IS looking down on us from his home on the first floor of No. 1 Cambridge Terrace in this picture. William James Duncan Best, Justice of the Peace and member of the Royal College of Surgeons, lived here between about 1896 and 1922. His wife, Ellen, and their children, Cecil, Leslie and Eileen, also lived here, as did a nurse, a housekeeper and a cook.

The tram lines and the telegraph cables criss-crossing the scene offer hints to its age. The buildings are Grade II listed, being mid-nineteenth-century constructions; they are stuccoed (plastered) to the front and ends, with bare brick to the rear.

We don't know where Dr Best moved to from here, but we know that he died on 1 May 1926, in Folkestone, at the age of sixty-three.

THE TELEGRAPH WIRES and the trams rails are long gone now, and the buildings are part of a familiar scene – one usually filled with smelly, noisy trucks as they go to and from the Eastern Docks. The Hotel de France stood not far from here in the 1970s, and if still there today would be right in the middle of the new road.

Unfortunately most of Cambridge Terrace is now empty, and all the windows have been boarded up, although part of Dr Best's house is now a restaurant. In 1992 a famous Bronze Age boat was found under this section of road. The boat dates back 3,500 years and is the oldest seagoing vessel ever found.

DOVER CASTLE

MOST OF US don't get to survey our town from the air – let alone from the air of the 1950s! We could write masses on what's on view here, but shall content ourselves with pointing out a few things.

Between the castle keep and the castle church is a Victorian married quarters; behind, and to the left of the 1858 Officers' Mess (below the church mound), are other barrack blocks and associated

buildings. Right in front of the 1858 Officers' Mess is the nineteenth-century military hospital, and in front of that, on the cliff edge, is the Admiralty Lookout. And – last but not least – to the far right is the old East Arrow Barracks, built in the 1920s. That will do – though we could go on for ages!

MANY OF THE buildings we mentioned in the 1950s picture have now gone, mostly demolished in the 1950s and '60s as they were obsolete after the Army left the castle. The East Arrow Barracks finally went in the early 1980s. Luckily, however, the Admiralty Lookout has been kept. It has since been conserved and restored to such a standard that it is now possible to visit it.

Of course there are obvious changes elsewhere. The seafront and esplanade area is vastly different, as is the port, and the trees seem to take over where brickwork once ruled. I don't suppose much else in this view can change now – as we all probably know, the Eastern Docks can't be enlarged any further.

CASTLE STREET

THIS MUST BE early in the morning as there is no one about in this view of Castle Street. On the frontage of Calver's shop on the left there is a very impressive array of adverts. They are, from left to right, Spratt's Patent Dog Cakes and Chicken Meal, Simpson's Calf Meals (the 'Best & Cheapest'), Spratt's Parrot Food, Spratt's Patent Terrier Biscuits, and Thorley's Food for Cattle. The rest are out of focus. I particularly like the selection of newspapers outside Mr Calver's

shop. Going up the street from Calver's in 1909, we find the premises of William Eastes, corn, hay and straw merchant and farmer; after this, we come to May Mercer's milliner; J. Austen, a cycle agent and repairer; Mrs Hodgson, certified midwife, and A. Woodham's Imperial Dairy.

BEFORE CASTLE STREET was built in the 1830s the honour of being the main artery across town went to St James's Street. The buildings have hardly changed since that time. Next time you walk down there, look up and you'll see remains of William Eastes' sign! Calver's store has very recently become a branch of Martin & Co. Letting Agents.

MORE CASTLE STREET

HERE'S ANOTHER NICE view looking along Castle Street. You can just see A. Calver's shop up on the left. There are three corners here – most prominently Flashman's, 'Upholsterer to the Queen and His Royal Highness'. Flashman sold insurance, was an estate agent, auctioneer, property valuer, decorator, furnisher, a house removals and storage provider and, last but not least, a funeral director! This business was established in 1830.

On the opposite side are the former stables for the Antwerp Hotel, later to become Hubbard's Umbrella Manufactory, a building which was destroyed – along with the adjacent Pickfords' removal depot – during the last shelling of Dover on 26 September 1944.

FOLLOWING THE DESTRUCTION of the buildings in the Second World War, the site was later to become home to the showrooms of Martin Walter's garage (in the building that can be seen here covered in scaffolding). Later on, the building was to become a branch of the Trustee Savings Bank (or TSB) and was most recently converted to the 'Dover Gateway', providing face-to-face services from both Kent County Council and Dover District Council.

In the foreground is the fountain, here covered over for the winter season. Sadly, due to budget cuts, a less attractive and cheaper replacement is soon to be installed.

PIER DISTRICT AND WESTERN HEIGHTS

THERE IS FAR too much to mention in this early picture of the area known as Archcliffe. Only three structures in this picture are still present today. To the top left we see the 1858 Officers' Mess in the Western Heights' Citadel, which is now part of an immigration removal centre. To the top right we can see the back of the Victoria Hall, used as a regimental institute and latterly as a social club for the prison officers of the borstal, which is now partially burnt out. The remains of Archcliffe Fort are hard to pick out of this busy picture, but it is roughly to the left of the long row of terraced houses constituting Beach Street.

Above the fort is the long-gone RASC yard, and above that a row of Edwardian married quarters. Above those, shoe-horned into the hill, we can see the South Front Barracks, demolished in 1959.

THIS AREA WAS changed forever in the early 1960s as most of the land and buildings were sold off to the local authority. The buildings were demolished and small factories were built. Channel House, P&O's headquarters, was built adjacent to the 1960s Racole Ladder Factory building. The site of the barracks became a coal yard, amongst other things, and the company we know today as Megger was built on the greatest proportion of the land, their humble beginnings in 1965 being a converted stable block.

Archcliffe Fort is now worth a visit to rifle through antiques and second-hand books in the St Emmaus charity community shopping centre. At the time of writing it has been proposed that a housing estate be built on the skyline. Once again, time will tell.

CLARENCE LAWN

AN EXTRACT FROM *The Book of the Burlington, Dover*, compiled in around 1928 and written by Lt-Col Newnham Davis, food critic and gourmet, reads thus:

> *The Hotel Burlington, Dover is situated on the Marine Parade. Full south aspect, overlooking the Promenade, Prince of Wales, Admiralty and East Piers, and commanding magnificent views of the Channel. Sheltered from the north and east winds. The Hotel is fitted with the latest sanitary improvements and is most luxuriously appointed throughout by Maple. Hydraulic passenger and luggage lifts. During winter the Hotel is warmed by patent radiators.*
>
> *A unique feature of the Hotel is the Oriental Lounge, situated on the ground floor, containing fine specimens of Indian Arcading. Here the Burlington Orchestra plays selections during the afternoons and evenings, Sundays included.*

UNFORTUNATELY THIS ONCE dignified building, with its decorative Italianate tower, was severely damaged by shelling during the Second World War. The shelling didn't totally destroy it, but it was damaged enough to be pulled down. The current site is now rather less inviting, comprising a petrol filling station, some scrub land and part of the A20 dual carriageway that cuts the town from the seafront. The bust in Clarence Lawn is, of course, of Captain Matthew Webb, the first person to successfully swim the English Channel; he made his record attempt in 1875. He died in 1883 in an attempt to swim the rapids below the Niagara Falls.

CROSSWALL

THIS IS ONE half of a stereoview image dating back to the 1860s. It shows the long-since removed clock tower and wind vane tower that were situated on either side of the Crosswall leading into the Granville Dock. Designed by James Moon, the resident engineer and harbour master, they were constructed in 1830 and 1831 respectively. In 1877 both towers were removed as the harbour expanded outwards, but the clock was incorporated into the current clock tower at the base of the Prince of Wales Pier.

THE CROSSWALL HAS seen a lot of industries and businesses come and go, including P. Campbell Bushell & Co., fuel agent, and the LC&SER Stores, but the area is currently home to George Hammond PLC, a company who offer motorboats for hire, on the western side and the RNLI lifeboat station on the eastern side. The current lifeboat station moved to the new building in 2001 from a site near the Marine Station. The Granville Dock is separated from the tidal basin by the Granville Bridge and both are now very popular leisure-boat berths.

DOVER BAY

THIS RELATIVELY MODERN view, taken from the saluting battery at the castle, dates back to the 1960s but still varies from today's vista. The Western Docks hoverport and the Burlington House tower block are yet to be built, and the Grand Shaft Barracks on the Western Heights are still standing but soon to be demolished. At this time the Eastern Docks' roll-on roll-off ferries had only been operating for a few years and Townwall Street is still quite a small thoroughfare. You will just be able to make out the Hotel de France in the middle of what is now the A20.

THESE IMAGES ARE separated by about fifty years. The first 'ro-ro' freight came to Dover in 1965 and the service now carries 2 million lorries per year (2011 figures). Nearly 5 million vehicles and 13 million passengers now pass through the town to cross the English Channel every year.

MARKET SQUARE

DOES THIS 1934 snapshot show a friend of the photographer, or is it just a local resident moving from playing billiards in the Walmer Castle pub towards the Prince Regent public house a few doors down? The prominent arches on the right are part of the current Dover Museum and former indoor market. The museum opened in this building in 1849, but moved temporarily to Maison Dieu House after the last war. This temporary move turned out to last over forty years!

THE MODERN MUSEUM building was built behind the Grade II listed arched façade in 1991 to house a modern museum and, in 1999, a new extension was added to show the Bronze Age boat which had then just recently been discovered under Townwall Street. Work is currently taking place to extend the foyer of the museum into the arches to allow the relocation of the Tourist Information Centre, which is presently located in an out-of-the-way location at the old town gaol. The £150,000 project was completed in August 2012.

EAST CLIFF

THE RATHER ELEGANT building perched on the top of the cliff (top right) is part of the East Arrow Barracks complex that sprung up in 1927. Somewhat curiously, the redundant Langdon Barracks – formerly a convict prison, demolished in 1925 – provided the bricks for East Arrow Barracks. They were transported across the valley on a purpose-built narrow-gauge rail system.

An early form of recycling? The chalk scarring that can be seen on the right has been made by workers creating 'one of the finest parade grounds in the country' for the garrisoned soldiers. In the bay we can see the old Promenade Pier in the process of being demolished, which conveniently gives us a date of May or June 1927 for this photograph.

THESE NEW BARRACKS survived right into the 1980s after failing to be sold by the Ministry of Defence. There is a nice headline in the local paper of 1966: 'Who wants to buy a barracks?!' Today's scene is far less serene – all docks and dual carriageway. When it was opened in 1977 the Jubilee-Way viaduct carried on over the water, but with continual dock expansion it is now entirely over the land.

41

No. 167 SNARGATE STREET

No. 167 SNARGATE Street seems to have been a draper's shop by as early as 1889. Prior to 1891, Mr Walter Greey traded here. The chap we see here, Ernest Everett, was here from around 1895 to about 1899. It looks like the next draper here was Mr E.W. Lawrence. Mr Lawrence moved to the site in 1901, and was here for approximately twenty years. H.L. Lawrence then had the premises for the run up to the Second World War.

As an aside, the photographer was Alexander Grossman. Alexander traded from various addresses in

Snargate Street between 1862 and 1898, when he went bankrupt. Perhaps competition from the numerous other photographers in the area forced him out of business?

THE MODERN BUILDING that now stands at No. 167 Snargate Street is, I think you'll agree, not quite as interesting as Ernest's shop. It would appear that his shop was long gone by 1950, and its removal from the landscape was possibly a result of enemy action. To the right you can see another view of the building which housed Mrs Metcalf's Bon Marché store.

STROND STREET

LOOKING DOWN ON the Strond Street area, this image could date from as far back as the 1850s, as the South Eastern Railway and the London Chatham & Dover Railway lines are yet to join via the Harbour Tunnel, which opened in 1861. The most prominent features are Holy Trinity church, the Crosswall towers and the Admiralty Pier (which is here at an early stage

of construction). Part of the Pier District, the area was the site of hundreds of homes and countless pubs. However, these were considered to be slum buildings, and were cleared from as early as the 1920s. Through organised slum clearance, bombings and expansion of the Western Docks, only a handful of historic buildings remain in this area, including the Lord Warden Hotel.

IF PLANS FOR 'Dover Terminal 2' come to fruition this view will change beyond recognition. The Granville Dock and tidal harbours will be infilled to create parking for the cross-Channel traffic. The end of the Prince of Wales Pier will be lopped off to build new ferry berths and allow manoeuvring room for the ships. The Wellington Dock would be landlocked and the marina moved to the inside of the Prince of Wales Pier. This is all dependent on traffic, the volume of which is currently at a standstill due to the worldwide economic climate. The site of the hoverport can also be seen – it lasted from 1978 until its demolition in 2009.

PRINCE OF WALES PIER

LOOKING ALONG THE Prince of Wales Pier, the first thing that one notices is the gap in the terrace with the ornate metalwork, the ironwork presumably more for building support than decoration. The gap was created when the new Wellington Bridge brought the railway onto the pier to serve the Atlantic liners that berthed here. Separated to the left is the Esplanade Hotel, which offered 'Hot and Cold Baths, Electric Light and Excellent Cuisine with inclusive terms from 7s 6d per day or from 35s per week according to the season.'

WHEN THE HOVERPORT for the cross-Channel hovercraft moved from the Eastern Docks into its own purpose-built base at the Western Docks in the 1970s, the open ironwork of the pier was concreted in, changing its appearance totally. If Dover Terminal 2 is built the current marina will be landlocked. Two suggestions are to build a new marina on the outside of the pier accessed from the beach, or to create a new cutting between Wellington Dock and the seafront.

SNARGATE STREET

THIS PICTURE TAKES us back to a time when there was still shipbuilding, fishing and associated trades in Dover. This is Wellington Dock, which is more important than we all probably realise as it still retains the rough footprint of the Great Pent, Dover's original harbour, which can be seen on maps of Dover since 1595. If you walk around the dock today you'll still see some interesting *objet d'ock*, so to speak, such as early nineteenth-century bollards, mooring rings and other interesting ironwork. Bussey's, Mowll and Hawksfield's coal stores occupied numerous buildings around the quay when this shot was taken. It was also home to Bert Cullin, shipbuilder, Sharp and Enright's sailmaker's, Dover Harbour Board Engineering Depot and, at one time, Lambert & Weston, photographers.

TODAY SOME OF the quay has been filled in to provide car parking, and the boat sheds are now full of clothes, shoes, books and ornaments in the form of De Bradlie Wharf Shopping Outlet (which utilised some of the old sheds).

As you will see, the seaward side buildings of Snargate Street are entirely missing, some as a result of Second World War bombing – such as the Hippodrome Theatre, which can just be seen in the bottom right of the older image – and others through various road-widening projects over the years.

As part of redevelopment plans it is proposed that the base station of the cable car from the castle is re-located to the car park at the centre of the image, along with another leading up to the Western Heights. A land bridge passing over the roundabout is also proposed to create another connection between the town and seafront – at the moment, the dual carriageway effectively cuts the town in two.

KING STREET

THE SHADES ARE pulled down on some of these shops and the shadows are growing tall on this sunny day in King Street in 1911. Some shop names are visible on this picture, namely H. Underdown, who sold books, papers, general and fancy stationery; he was also a printer, engraver, sportsmen's outfitter, looking-glass and picture-frame manufacturer, artist's repository – and much more!

These businesses were all present in this part of King Street too in 1911: Deal and Walmer Coalfield and Kent Coal League, temporary premises for the United Collieries' Museum, Rapid Art Photography Studios (trade name of Arthur Burger), Opera Sweeteries, the general post office and the office of the superintendent of Royal Mail Packets.

ISN'T IT NICE that some of these buildings still remain (albeit with some of their architectural ornamentation removed or covered over)? The highly impressive old Labour Exchange is still empty and is currently up for auction, no buyer having been found. Wasn't it tidier without cars!?

MARINE PARADE

A BOOK ABOUT Dover is bound to have more than a few seaside pictures, and here's another one from the turn of the century. Here too is the building that was later to house the Royal Cinque Ports Yacht Club. The club, the fifth oldest Royal yacht club in England, was founded in 1872

and moved to its present location following the destruction of the original club premises by enemy gunfire in 1940. It was formerly located on the seafront near the entrance to the Promenade Pier, which can just be seen in this photograph.

THE TWO STONE edifices on the seafront here are a memorial to swimmers, entitled *On the Crest of a Wave*. The piece was commissioned in 1995 by the Dover Harbour Board and created by Ray Smith: it has been described as 'two white blocks of Portland Stone rising from a bed of textured sea green Kirkstone slate. From the top of the rocks can be seen two profiles of swimmers pushing forward into the rising wave of the stones and cut from a similar dark green slate.'

A landmark sculpture on a prime site, it is a part of Kent County Council's Town Centres' Initiative public art project.

MARINE STATION

PLATFORM FIVE IS empty as we stand on the pedestrian bridge just inside the Marine Station and look in the direction of the new cruise-ship terminus. Dover Cruise Terminal 1, as it is now known, was built prior to the First World War and was used for military rail movements. It reopened after the war, in 1918, as the South Eastern & Chatham Railway terminus.

This area of Dover was the centre of rail activities for many years. Indeed, the famous Golden Arrow service would arrive and depart from this railway station until it ceased operation in the 1980s. Rail activities finished for good at the station in 1994 and the building remained in a derelict state until it was converted into a cruise terminal.

TODAY THE BUILDING doubles as a car park and a waiting room/reception area for cruise-liner passengers. There are currently plans to spend £10 million on the structure. This will include a new roof complete with glazing, and repairs to masonry, steelwork and windows.

Inside, at the far end of the station, is the First World War memorial to the South Eastern & Chatham railwaymen who lost their lives in that conflict. Unfortunately there is no public access to this memorial or building.

MARKET SQUARE

A SUNNY DAY in Market Square during the early 1960s. Do you remember this scene before the street was pedestrianized? The post-Second World War architecture – 'shoebox' buildings – seem to dominate the Victorian charm of this busy junction. At least the Burlington House office block isn't built yet.

Do we all remember Phillips Pleasing Outfitters, Liverpool Victoria Insurances Offices, Pearl Wallpaper Co., East Kent Electronics, and Pelosi's? The bus spotters among us will already know that the 129 bus went to St Radigunds.

LITTLE HAS CHANGED here in fifty years. In a controversial move, it was agreed that Market Square would become the site for one of the twenty-two 'Olympic' big-screen televisions. These span the UK, from Plymouth, Norwich, Dover and Edinburgh to Belfast.

MARKET SQUARE

HERE IS A good example of the Victorian charm of the old Market Square mentioned on the previous page! Amongst the many advertisements for alcohol – the Leney Brewery adverts on the trams, the Carlton Club on the left and the Garrick's Head awaiting its patrons – there is also something here for the teetotallers: the International Tea Co. Stores!

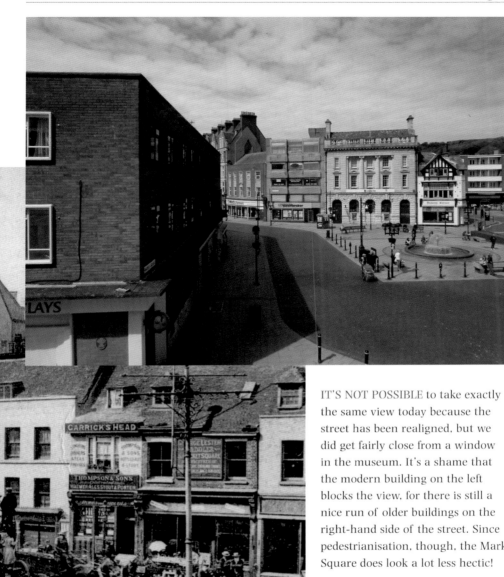

IT'S NOT POSSIBLE to take exactly the same view today because the street has been realigned, but we did get fairly close from a window in the museum. It's a shame that the modern building on the left blocks the view, for there is still a nice run of older buildings on the right-hand side of the street. Since pedestrianisation, though, the Market Square does look a lot less hectic!

NEW BRIDGE

TURNING AROUND FROM the earlier view of Cambridge Terrace is this view looking along New Bridge towards Bench Street. It was taken in around 1908. On the left are the Granville Club and Prudential Assurance Co. offices, later to become the Hotel de France and the Shakespeare Hotel, and on the right W. & R. Fletcher, butcher's, and the Day Star Book Room. It is assumed that the Day Star Book Room was connected to the Day Star Mission in Durham Hill and the Day Star Home of Rest on the Esplanade, a hotel for Christian workers. Note the amazing perambulator being pushed through the area which is now the A20 dual carriageway.

SADLY, MOST OF the traffic heading into Dover from the Folkestone direction passes past this row of derelict buildings and building sites. The former hotel and later amusement arcade stand empty, as does the adjacent site of the Crypt Restaurant. There are no buildings between Bench Street and Burlington House: all have been systematically demolished over the past ten years.

Fortunately, however, land has been purchased and planning permissions put in place for the empty sites around St James's Street, so hopefully this area will also be incorporated into any redevelopment of the area.

DOVER CASTLE

NEXT TO THE very familiar keep and curtain walls are the Victorian married soldiers' quarters on Palace Green – named after Palace Gate, which leads into the keep yard. The castle was home to many hundreds of men of the Royal Garrison Artillery that manned the guns around Dover.

This accommodation block along with many other redundant buildings were demolished in the 1950s and '60s, when the military pulled out of the castle. However, the

set of tunnels known as DUMPY were home to a Cold War Regional Seat of Government until 1984. Today Constable's Tower is home to the only garrisoned soldier in the town of Dover, Brigadier Simon Wolsey.

IN 2009 A multi-million pound project was completed to revamp and rebrand the keep as the Great Tower. Away went the displays of Henry VIII – we are now taken back to the late twelfth century and the time of Henry II. Accurate furnishings and colourful wall hangings have been reinstalled to bring the so-called 'Dark Ages' to life. An estimated £2 million has been spent on the secret wartime tunnels as part of the new Dunkirk Evacuation interpretation.

PROMENADE PIER

REGATTA DAY DURING the 1920s can't have been so different from the Dover Regatta we all enjoy today. There were ice creams, boat trips and a huge turnout of people to enjoy the sun and the fun. This Promenade Pier view looks across Clarence Lawn to the Burlington Hotel in the distance. On the left we can see the dance hall of Granville Gardens, and in the background the majestic curves of Camden Terrace.

The pier was opened in 1893 by the mayor's wife, Mrs Dickeson, with a pavilion being added in 1901. It was 940ft long, which included a landing stage for

paddle-steamers to dock. The pier was a popular venue at which to roller skate and listen to music and for seeing variety acts, amongst whom we find Harold Montague and his music-hall troupe, who were known as 'The Vagabonds' Entertainment', and the celebrated Miss Esme Atherden.

THE MODERN-DAY Dover Regatta is still fun and (mostly) sun! Modern activities include Dragon-Boat racing, Newfoundland rescue dogs on display, helicopter rides, Air-Sea Rescue displays, a food market, fireworks, bands, a funfair, and displays by the impressive RNLI offshore and inshore lifeboats.

PRINCES STREET

THIS INTERESTING IMAGE from the 1930s shows Princes Street Garage which was home, when this photograph was taken, to Mr J. Walker's garage and Mr E. Stanley, an electrical wiring contractor; Mr Stanley also operated from the building. Perhaps one of them is standing outside their premises posing for this photograph? To the right edge can be seen the end of the burial ground for St Martin-le-Grand church, the ruins of which can now be seen adjacent to the Dover Discovery Centre in the Market Square.

In 1901, Bavington-Jones referred to No. 4, the building next door, as 'home of the Good Shepherd, conducted by Miss Hoare, which has a laundry to give work to the inmates. This institution, which seeks to raise fallen women, is as worthy of support as any of the religious houses that in ages past have flourished in this locality.'

DURING THE SECOND World War, Dover, a front-line town, was subjected to a large number of bombing raids and to shelling from the German cross-Channel guns on the French coast. As the Allies closed in on the Pas de Calais area in late 1944, the rate of fire from those guns intensified before they were finally captured. The buildings shown may have been destroyed during the night of 14 and 15 September 1944, when No. 5 Princes Street and an adjoining store suffered a direct hit. As there appear to have been no casualties, few details were recorded.

MARINE PARADE

THIS PHOTOGRAPH IS possibly of another Dover Regatta day. People seem to be ignoring the 'concert' advert on the gates of the Promenade Pier and are walking by. Although the pier offered roller skating and musical entertainment, its commercial existence was threatened by the same type of entertainment being available at Granville Gardens, where row after row of deck chairs were lined up in front of the little pavilion there, and also by the skating that could be enjoyed at the Dover Skating Rink just down the road, not far from East Cliff.

The ornately decorated entrance kiosks, with their 'onions' on the top, controlled entrance to the pier; there were also six iron gates. The electric lights were added in 1901 when the pavilion was built at the end of the pier. Prior to that, the pier's handrails doubled as gas pipes to carry gas to the lights which illuminated its length.

RATHER THAN SHOW you another view of the seafront, we thought it would be far more fun to show you what remains of the pier's fittings!

As a result of commercial difficulties suffered by the Promenade Pier and Pavillion Co. Ltd, the pier was sold to the Admiralty in 1913 for £8,000, and was finally demolished in 1927. In July of that year two auctions were held in which fixtures and fitting were sold off. The items for sale included the lead work from the roofs and gutters, metal piping, electrical conduits, copper wiring, a 9ft-diameter glass dome and – last but not least – the six metal entrance gates that guarded the seafront entrances. They were bought for an unknown sum, but travelled all the way to Maidstone – where they carried on guard duty, though now as entrance gates to Pope's Hall Farm. Of the six gates only two remain today, the other four (according to the owner) having been 'melted down during the Second World War to build Spitfires and Hurricanes!'

SALEM CHURCH, BIGGIN STREET

WEDNESDAY, 22 SEPTEMBER 1909 was the unveiling date of two foundation stones for the new Sunday school behind the Salem Baptist church in Biggin Street. Strangely this photograph was taken through Tolputt's Timber Yard, which was situated behind the church (as can be seen by the stacks of wood to the right of the picture). The stone was unveiled by the former president of the Baptist Union, the Revd Principal W.J. Henderson BA of Bristol, along with many other clergy from all over Kent.

THE CHURCH (and the attached Sunday school) was purchased in 1975 by Boots the Chemist and subsequently demolished to build the store that still stands today. It replaced smaller Boots stores that were elsewhere in the main street. What became of the various foundation stones we do not know, but five of the memorial stones were moved to the new chapel in Maison Dieu Road. All that remains in Biggin Street is a small section of façade between the chemist and adjacent shoe shop, and allegedly some vaults remain under the pavement in front of the store.

MARINE PARADE

THIS EXTREMELY CLEAR image dates from the 1880s and shows the seafront complete with the rows of Georgian terraces that stretched between the eastern and western docks. Nearest to the photographer is the building of the new swimming baths: this had opened just a few years earlier, in 1878, and allowed the less-adventurous to swim indoors in seawater rather than take a bathing machine on the beach opposite. The smartly dressed lad looks to be holding a towel, perhaps to tempt in a passing tourist!

ALL OF THE buildings to the right of the gas lamp were victims of shelling and bombing of the town in the Second World War. The only building that survived was Marine Court, to the left of the baths. This, however, was controversially demolished in the 1990s by Dover Harbour Board. Its replacement was the modern hotel which is now home to the Premier Inn hotel and restaurant chain.

EAST CLIFF

THIS RARE IMAGE shows the three aircraft hangars and the slipway of the Royal Naval Air Station which was situated below the Georgian casemates of Dover Castle. The small site has had a very busy history, having been the site of the eighteenth-century Guilford Battery – which was demolished in 1909 to make way for Dover's first skating rink and the world's first open-air cinema! In 1914 the site was requisitioned by the RNAS (Royal Naval Air Service) who converted the roller-skating rink building (seen on the far left) into shed one and soon after added sheds two and three next door.

WITH THE RNAS becoming part of the Royal Air Force by combining with the Royal Flying Corps in 1918, the site was redundant within a few years. Sheds two and three were demolished in the 1920s. The former rink was used by the Cinque Ports Anti-Aircraft Regiment in the Second World War, and remained in use as a drill hall until it was demolished in the 1980s. All that now remains on the site of the hangars is a brick building, last used as an Army recruitment office, and an old boat shed (a modern construction). The brick building was part of the Guilford Battery and possibly dates to around 1780, but has stood empty for over ten years and really wants rescuing before it totally collapses due to its ruinous state.

SHAKESPEARE CLIFF

NO MATTER THE age of the photograph, one can always rely on Shakespeare Cliff to look impressive! Archcliffe Road was a country lane when this photograph was taken. This sailor may have thought he'd never visit Dover again and wanted his photograph taken for posterity, with the cliff as an impressive backdrop! He is steadying himself on War Department fencing (the same type still at Dover Castle today), this whole area being part of the Western Heights complex at that time. The familiar railway tunnels are there and just above, on the cliff top by the allotments, is the Spion Kop radio station, presumably named after the Battle of Spion Kop (which took place during the Second Boer War in January 1900).

LIKE THE CASTLE, we can rely on Shakespeare Cliff and the twin railway tunnels to provide a backdrop of continuity to the ever-changing face of Dover. Where our sailor had his portrait taken is now a noisy, smelly truck route, and the military fencing has been replaced with concrete. Old Ray Langabeer's corner shop, Sunny Corner, has been and gone.

TOWN FROM THE
WESTERN HEIGHTS

LOOKING FROM THE Western Heights near the Drop Redoubt we can see all the way across town, and we're on a level with Victoria Park. Below, in the valley, this 1890s photograph shows the hotchpotch of houses and shops, which make for a very busy photograph. York Street can be seen, as can the many churches that used to populate the Victorian skyline of the town. Who can spot St Mary's, New St James', Old St James', and St Mary in Castro?

FOLLOWING EARLIER SLUM clearance and bombing, this area was to change forever in the 1970s when the York Street dual carriageway carved through between Folkestone Road and Snargate Street.

The interestingly named Cause is Altered public house is now long gone, and quite a few roads too – including Hartley Street, Portland Place, Union Row, Blucher Street and Durham Place. Thankfully, after a lot of campaigning, the level of the new York Street was raised in order to protect the remains of the Roman Classis Brittanica (British fleet) fort that lies not too far below the surface.

SNARGATE STREET

THIS IMAGE FROM the early 1900s shows Snargate Street, which, as you all know, was one of the main thoroughfares between the town and the old Pier District. It was frequented by merchants and military men alike and contained many pubs and churches. As well as Bottle and Gandy, and Langley's, both grocers, the largest building which still stands is Mrs Metcalf's Bon Marché. A general trader, Mrs Metcalf sold books, heraldic china, fancy and leather goods to the public.

MANY OF THE buildings in the street were victims of bombing in the Second World War, an era which also saw the destruction of the Hippodrome theatre (situated behind the photographer). More buildings were destroyed in the 1970s, including the Dover Express offices, demolished when York Street was constructed. Hopefully the next big change will be to the Burlington House tower block, a building which currently stands empty and awaiting demolition for the Dover Town Investment Zone works in the St James' area.

CUSTOM HOUSE QUAY

THE HARBOUR OF yesteryear was arguably far more interesting than it is today. This photograph, from the early twentieth century, portrays a busy harbour area down in the Pier District. We can see Pickford's warehouse, and, on the right, more warehouses on Custom House Quay next to the now-disappeared Strond Street. In the middle-centre distance is the Royal Military Hospital, built in around 1805 and thus contemporary with the Drop Redoubt and Grand Shaft. Above

that are the South Front Barracks, set into the hillside below the old soldiers' married quarters. To the far right, on the cliff top, is Victoria Hall, the one-time regimental institute for men stationed on the Western Heights.

TODAY THE NUMBER of boats in the marina is impressive. These make the area look quite pretty, but many of the built structures are long gone. This is mostly due to demolition and redevelopment rather than enemy action, sad to say. The military hospital and barracks were cleared in 1963 and 1959, respectively, to make way for new factories, and Victoria Hall was gutted by fire about a decade ago.

PRINCE OF WALES PIER

THE PRINCE OF WALES PIER was completed in 1902, and a railway track was soon laid along its length to serve the berths at its far end. For a few years Dover became the port of call for huge cruise liners of the Hamberg America Line, whose ship the SS *Pennsylvania* can be seen here. The *Pennsylvania* was built by Harland & Wolff (who also built *Titanic*), and was launched in 1896. The ship served with the US Navy in the First World War but was scrapped in 1924.

ON COMPLETION OF the Southern Breakwater and Admiralty Pier extension, however, the pier became unsuitable for such large ships. Here you can see the café that was built to replace 'The Lighthouse Restaurant'. That was destroyed in the great storm of 1987. If plans for the development and enlargement of Terminal 2 come to fruition, the pier head could be removed to allow manoeuvring room for ferries and for several new berths.

OLD ST JAMES'S CHURCH

ST JAMES'S CHURCH is thought to be one of Dover's oldest churches and stands next door to what is probably Dover's oldest pub, the White Horse. Almost certainly referred to in the Domesday Book, the church was of Saxon origin, although the present ruin dates to the 1100s.

As well as a congregational meeting place, the church was also used by the courts of the barons of the Cinque Ports. The Victorians decided that St James' was too small, and New St James' church was built in 1860 in Maison Dieu Road, the old church being restored in 1869.

WHAT REMAINS OF the church today is less than a shell. Enemy action in the last war took its toll, although there are some interesting areas to look at within the walls still. The churchyard next door was removed following an archaeological excavation in 1973 and the leisure centre and its car park now occupy the spot. Trevannion Street, which led to the church, is now just a car park.

ST MARY IN CASTRO

ST MARY IN CASTRO is one of the finest Saxon buildings in Kent and stands on what is thought to be the site of an Iron Age hillfort. It was constructed, it is thought, by reusing Roman material from the nearby Roman Pharos (or lighthouse). By the early eighteenth century it was in a state of decay and used as a coal store, and even as a sports court, for the Castle Garrison. In this photograph the major restoration work by Sir Gilbert Scott has been carried out and the church is again usable.

DESPITE THE EARLIER restoration, it was not until the work in the 1880s by William Butterfield that the church tower was competed and the polychromatic tiling added to the walls inside. The church is still consecrated and used for regular services, including the installation of Lord Wardens. Today it is possible to get married in the church if one is in the Armed Forces.

ST MARY'S CHURCH

AN INTERESTING VIEW of the parish church of St Mary. The terrace on the right commenced construction as part of a road-widening project. This period also saw the demolition of the Antwerp Hotel which was just off to the right of the picture. In the background you can see

Longley's Star Inn, which was run by Dover's famous forty-two stone landlord Thomas Longley in an area that is now the Stembrook car park.

TODAY'S PHOTOGRAPH IS from a slightly different angle, as the site opposite was empty when the earlier picture was taken. St Mary's today has many modern stained-glass windows. These replaced the originals, many destroyed during the Second World War. Today's windows commemorate the tragic sinking of the *Herald of Free Enterprise* in 1987 and the Air-Sea Rescue Service.

STROND STREET

THE CLASH OF 'modern' and ancient transport at the entrance
to Strond Street. The old horse and cart is met by the tram from
River heading into the Pier District. To the left is what looks like an
Austin 7. Trams are coming back but the horse-drawn cart is gone
forever. Behind can be seen Crundall's timber yard and the cranes of
Hawksfield's yard on the quayside. The trams came to Dover in 1897
and extended through the town, seafront and docks. The first tram
ran on 6 September 1897 and the last on 31 December 1936, the day
before the first East Kent Bus took over their routes.

ALTHOUGH STROND STREET still appears on maps of the town,
there are no standing buildings left and the road just passes through a
concrete hardstanding. There are kerb stones and a few cats-eyes still
there but other than that the area is now the Dover Marina, with a
busy boat-repair yard and the huge lifting cradle visible in this image.
Should the proposed Terminal 2 ferry terminal come to fruition, a
large roundabout and new viaduct are suggested to connect to (and
go over) the A20 on the left and follow the road across the Wellington
Bridge and into the new dock.
    Few reminders are left in Dover of the once-extensive tram system,
save the shelter in Folkestone Road, the sheds at Buckland and a small
stretch of line in Northampton Quay.

GRAND SHAFT
BARRACKS

THIS RUINED BARRACK block on the Western Heights is a victim of World War Three! The odd bomb did fall on the Heights in the two world wars, but the damage was caused to this, the Officers' Mess at Grand Shaft Barracks, during the making of the BBC film *The War Game*. The barracks were demolished as they were of no further use to the military, and the site was used by Peter Watkin, the film maker, during demolition in 1964. Today, we would call the film a 'docu-drama'. It was about life during a nuclear attack. The barracks were built around 1803 during the Napoleonic Wars. The Grand Shaft triple-helical staircase, for the movement of troops, and the Drop Redoubt fort were built nearby.

THE SITE IS now a public open space and is a haven for wildlife. Few architectural structures remain, save the actual Grand Shaft Staircases. Over the years there have been many proposals to reuse the space. Such proposals are often to build hotels, but the latest is for a National War Memorial to be constructed to commemorate the 1.7 million servicemen and women, merchant navy personnel and civilians who died in the service of this country in the First and Second World Wars. A hotel and visitor centre is also proposed on the Heights.

If you enjoyed this book, you may also be interested in…

Haunted Dover
LORRAINE SENCICLE

The historic Dover has had its fair share of waifs and strays travelling through it over the course of many years. The castle, pubs and the labyrinth of subterranean chambers under the famous white cliffs host a variety of ghouls and spectres. From the tale of the old woman in grey forever waiting for her last confession, to the ghost of Archbishop Geoffrey whose screams have been heard on stormy nights as he is dragged from Dover college to the castle, *Haunted Dover* provides a plethora of chilling tales; this spine-tingling book will fascinate anyone who dares to read it!

978 0 7524 4859 6

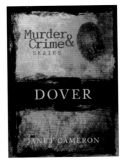

Dover Murder & Crime
JANET CAMERON

Those who fell foul of the law in Kent faced a horrible fate: some were thrown to their deaths from the top of Dover's white cliffs, whilst others were hanged, quartered, burnt or buried alive. Yet still the criminal fraternity of Kent went undeterred. This fascinating book contains tales of thwarted rivals and wicked soldiers, desperate mothers, licentious monks and disreputable women. With more than fifty illustrations, this chilling catalogue of murderous misdeeds is bound to captivate anyone interested in the criminal history of the area.

978 0 7524 3978 5

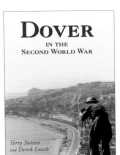

Dover in the Second World War
TERRY SUTTON AND DEREK LEACH

This book tells in detail what it was like to live in an English town constantly under siege from enemy guns in the Second World War. Many towns in Britain suffered from enemy action during the Second World War but none endured the almost daily explosions of shells fired from huge German guns on the French coast, some 21 miles away.

978 1 8607 7619 9

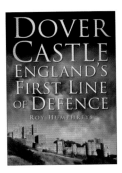

Dover Castle: England's First Line of Defence
ROY HUMPHREYS

The towering fortress of Dover Castle has stood as the gateway to England for many centuries, an imposing and, to an enemy at least, threatening sight. But on the high white cliffs and overlooking the Channel, from where it was intended to protect the coastline against attacks from Europe, the castle has always played an important part in the defence of Britain. Today it is regularly invaded by thousands of visitors keen to explore this dramatic and historic building. Dover Castle has undoubtedly played a major role in the defence of Britain since its earliest times, and here, Roy Humphreys describes the key role in this highly readble and well-illustrated book.

978 0 7524 5550 1

Visit our website and discover thousands of other History Press books.

www.thehistorypress.co.uk